A First Bilingual Dictionary

English/Bengali

SCHOFIELD & SIMS LIMITED, HUDDERSFIELD, ENGLAND

Pronunciation Guide

Most Asian languages are phonetic: every phoneme (unit of sound) is represented by a particular letter. One important feature of these languages is the articulation of the consonants **d** and **t**. These are always RETROFLEX consonants in the English language, but in the Asian languages they may be DENTAL consonants.

For example
The word **<u>d</u>arjan** ('dozen' in English) is pronounced with a softer dental **d**.
The word **bo<u>t</u>al** ('bottle' in English) is pronounced with a softer dental **t** .

RETROFLEX: the tongue rolls backwards and its tip touches the hard palate behind the teeth ridge.

retroflex

DENTAL: the tip of the tongue touches the inside of the upper teeth to produce a softer sound.

dental

Very many Asian words have dental consonants in them and if not correctly articulated, the pronunciation of the words is not only distorted, even the accuracy of the language may be lost.

In this book, since there are no equivalent dental consonants in the English language, where the **d**'s and **t**'s are to be pronounced DENTALLY they are <u>underlined</u> in the pronunciation guide.

A First Bilingual Dictionary

is available in five languages:

English/Bengali   0 7217 9500 5
English/Gujarati   0 7217 9501 3
English/Hindi   0 7217 9502 1
English/Punjabi   0 7217 9503 X
English/Urdu   0 7217 9504 8

© Schofield & Sims Ltd. 1995

0 7217 9500 5

First printed 1995

Design and typesetting by Armitage Typo/Graphics Ltd., Huddersfield
Translation and typesetting by Transindia, Slough

Printed and Bound in Italy by STIGE, Turin

Contents

The Body and Clothes

শরীর ও জামাকাপড়

shareer o jamakaapurd

ankle

গোড়ালী
gordali

apron

এইপরন্
aypran

arm

হাত
haath

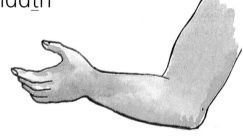

back

পিঠ
pith

badge

ব্যাজ
baej

belt

বেল্ট
baelt

4

blouse

ব্লাউজ্
blaaooz

boots

বুটস্
boots

buckle

বাক্‌ল
bakal

buttons

বাটনস্
batanz

cap

টুপি
tupi

cardigan

ক্যারডিগণ
kaardigan

cheek

গাল
gaal

chest

বুক
buk

chin
থুতনি
thoothni

coat
কোট
kot

dress
জামা
jaama

ear
কান
kaan

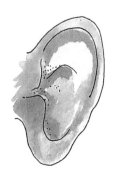

earring
কানের দুল
kaanayrdul

elbow
কুনুই
koonooi

eye
চোখ
chokh

eyebrow
ভুরু
bhooru

face

মুখ

mookh

finger

আঙ্গুল

aangul

foot

পায়ের পাতা

paayar paata

glasses

চশমা

chashma

gloves

দস্তানা

dastana

hair

চুল

chool

hand

হাত

haath

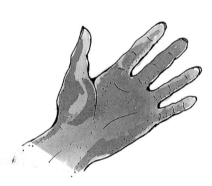

handkerchief

রুমাল

roomaal

hat
হ্যাট
haet

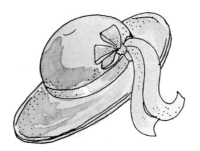

head
মাথা
maatha

helmet
হেলমেট্
haelmet

jacket
জ্যাকেট
jaakat

jeans
জীন
jeen

jumper
জ্যাম্পার
jampar

knee
হাটু
haatoo

laces
জুতোর ফিতে
jootar pheetay

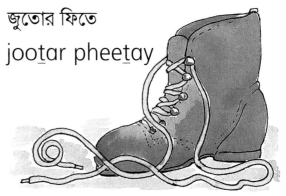

leg
পা
paa

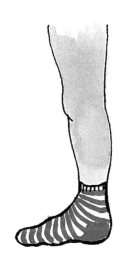

lips
ঠোঁট
tthot

mouth
হা মুখ
haamukh

nail
নখ
nakh

neck
গলা
gola

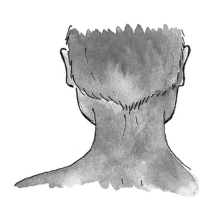

necklace
গলার হার
golar haar

nightdress
নাইট ড্রেস্
naaeet dress

nose
নাক
naak

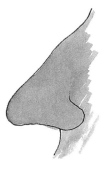

pocket
পকেট
paaket

purse
টাকা রাখার থলি
taka rakh
ṭholi

pyjamas
পায়জামা
paajama

ring
আঙটি
aangthee

sari
শাড়ী
shaardee

scarf
স্কার্ফ্
skaarf

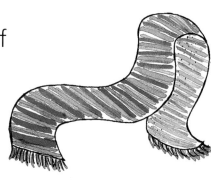

shalwar
সালোয়ার
shalwar

shirt
সার্ট
shaart

shoes
জুতো
jooto

sock
মোজা
moja

shorts
স্যরটস্
shorts

sweatshirt
সুঁয়েটসার্ট
sweatshaart

shoulder
কাঁধ
kaandh

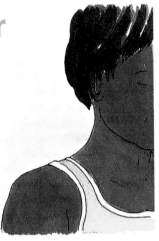

swimsuit
স্যুইম স্যুট
swimsoot

skirt
স্কার্ট
skart

teeth
দাঁত
daant

thumb

বুড়ো আঙুল

burdo
aangul

trainers

ট্রেইনার

traynarz

tie

টাই

taaee

trousers

ট্রাউজার

traaoozarz

tights

টাইটস্

taaeets

T-shirt

টি সার্ট

tee-shaart

tongue

জিব

jib

tummy

পেট

payt

turban
পাগড়ি
paagrdee

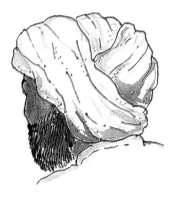

watch
হাতঘড়ি
haath ghardee

umbrella
ছাতা
chhaata

wellingtons
ওয়েলইংটনস্
waelingtanz

uniform
ইউনিফর্ম
uneefaarm

wrist
কব্জি
kubzee

vest
গেন্জি
gaynjee

zip
জ়িপ
jip

Home and Family

বাসস্হান ও পরিবার

baashas<u>t</u>haan o pareevar

baby
শিশু
shishoo

bandage
ব্যানডেইজ
baendayj

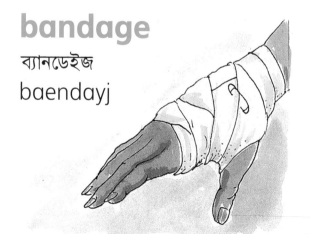

bath
ব্যাথ
baa<u>t</u>h

battery
ব্যাটারী
baetree

bed
বেড
baed

bell
ঘন্টা
ghantaa

book
বই
boee

bottle
বোতল
botal

bowl
গামলা
gaamla

boy
ছেলে
chhaylay

brother
ভাই
bhai

brush
ব্রাস
bursh

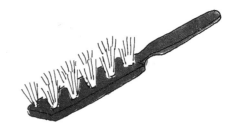

bucket
বালতি
baaltee

calendar
ক্যালেন্ডার
kaalandar

carpet
কার্পেট
kaarpat

clock
ঘড়ি
ghardee

chair
চেয়ার
chayar

cooker
কুকার
kukar

children
শিশুরা
shishoora

cup
কাপ
kap

chimney
চিমনি
chimnee

cupboard
তাকওয়ালা আলমারি
t̲aakwala
almaaree

curtains
পর্দা
pord_da

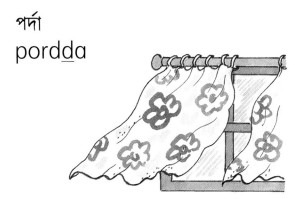

cushion
তাকিয়া
_takiya

daughter
কন্যা
kanya

dishwasher
ডিসওয়াসার
dishwaashar

door
দরজা
_dorja

drawer
দেরাজ
_daraaj

dustbin
ডাস্টবিন
dastbin

father
বাবা
baaba

fence
বেড়া
bayarda

garden
বাগান
baagaan

fire
আগুন
aagoon

gate
গেইট
gayt

floor
মেঝে
mayjha

girl
মেয়ে
maayae

garage
গ্যারাজ
gayraaj

glass
কাঁচ
kaanch

18

glue
আঠা
aattha

grandfather
পিতা বা মাতামহ
piṯa ba
maaṯa moho

grandmother
পিতা বা মাতামহী
piṯa ba
maaṯa mohi

hook
আঙটা
aangta

hose
নল
nal

house
বাড়ী
baardee

iron
ইস্ত্রি
isṯree

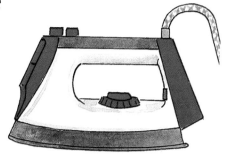

jug
জাগ
jag

kettle

কেটলি
kaytlee

key

চাবি
chaabee

knife

ছুরি
chhuree

ladder

মই
moee

lamp

ল্যাম্প
laemp

lawn

লন
laan

light bulb

লাইট বাল্ব
laaeet balb

magazine

ম্যাগাজিন
maegaazeen

man
পুরুষ
purash

match
দেশলাই
<u>d</u>iashalaaee

medicine
ঔষধ
osha<u>d</u>h

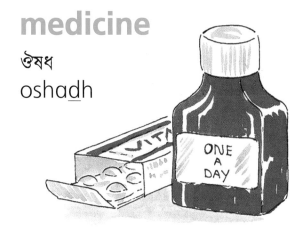

microwave
মাইক্রোওয়েভ
maaeekrowayv

mirror
আয়না
aaeena

money
টাকাপয়সা
taaka paisha

mother
মা
maa

mug
মগ
mag

needle
সুঁচ
chhoochh

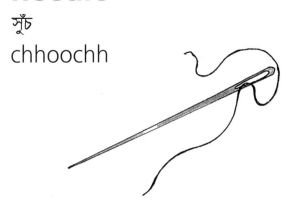

newspaper
খবরের কাগজ
khabray kaaghoz

paint
পেইন্ট
paynt

pan
প্যান্
paen

party
পার্টি
paartee

path
পথ
poth

pencil
পেনসিল
paensil

photograph
ফটোগ্রাফ
fotograaf

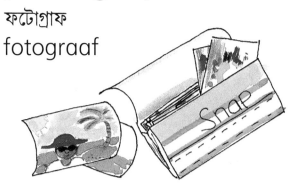

picture
ছবি
chhobee

pillow
বালিশ
baalish

pin
পিন
pin

plate
প্লেইট্
playt

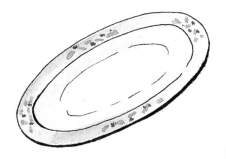

plug
প্লাগ
plag

quilt
লেপ
layp

radio
রেডিও
raydio

razor
রেজর
rayzar

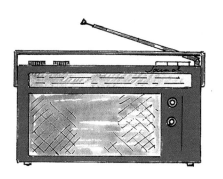

refrigerator

রেফ্রিজারেটর
raefrijaraytar

ruler

রুলার
roolar

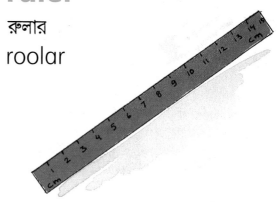

roof

ছাদ
chhat‍

saucer

পিরিচ
pirich

rubbish

আবর্জনা
aaborjana

scales

স্কেইল্স
skaylz

rug

রাগ
rag

scissors

কাঁচি
kaanchee

settee
সেটী
saetee

shed
শেড
shaed

shelf
শেল্‌ফ্‌
shaelf

shower
শাওয়ার
shaawar

sink
সিংক
sink

sister
বোন
bon

soap
সাবান
shaaban

son
পুত্র
putara

sponge
স্পনজ্
spanj

spoon
চামচে
chamchay

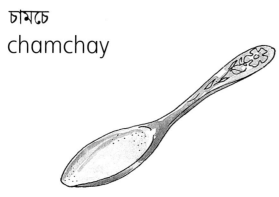

stairs
সিঁড়ি
sheerdee

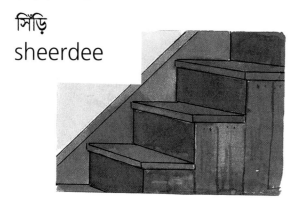

stool
স্টুল
stool

suitcase
স্যুটকেইস্
sootkays

table
টেবিল
taybil

tap
টেপ
taep

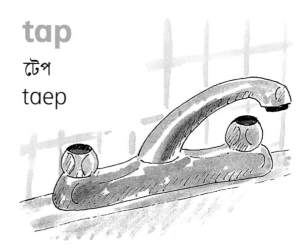

telephone
টেলিফোন
taeleefoon

television
টেলিভিশন
taeleeveezan

toilet
টয়লেট
taaylit

tent
তাবু
taaboo

toothbrush
টুথব্রাস
tuthbursh

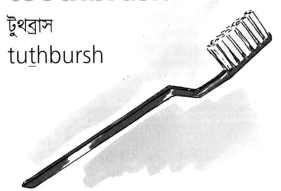

tin
টিন
tin

toothpaste
টুথ পেইল্ট
tuthpayst

toaster
টোস্টার
tostar

torch
টর্চ
torch

towel
তোয়ালে
toaalay

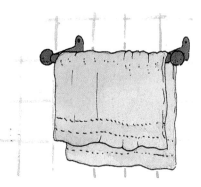

wedding
বিয়ে
biya

vacuum cleaner
ভেকুয়াম ক্লিনার
waekioom kleenar

window
জানালা
jaanala

video recorder
ভিডিও রেকর্ডার
vidio rikaardar

woman
নারী
naaree

washing-machine
ওয়াসিং মেশিন
waashing masheen

wool
উল
wool

Food and Drink

খাদ্য ও পানীয়

khaadhya o paanio

apple
আপেল
aapal

banana
কলা
kola

biscuit
বিস্কিট্
biskit

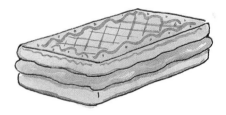

bread
রুটি
rotee

butter
মাখন
maakhan

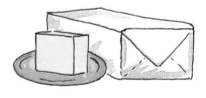

cabbage
বাধা কপি
baadha kopee

cake

কেইক্

kayk

carrot

গাজর

gaajor

cauliflower

ফুলকপি

phool kopee

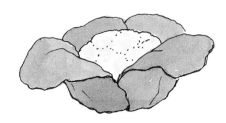

cereal

দানাশস্য

danashosho

chapatti

চাপাটি

chapaati

cheese

পনীর

poneer

cherry

চেরী

chayree

chocolate

চকলেট

choklayt

coffee

কফি
kofee

egg

ডিম
dim

cream

ক্রীম
kreem

fish

মাছ
maachh

crisps

ক্রিস্প্
krisp

flour

ময়দা
moaida

cucumber

শশা
shosha

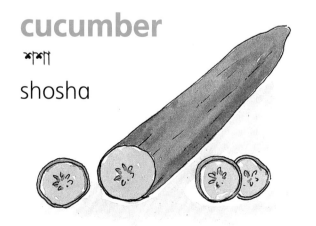

grapefruit

শরবতীলেবু
sharboteelayboo

grapes
আঙ্গুর
aangoor

jam
জ্যাম
jaem

hamburger
হামবারগার
haembargar

jelly
জেলী
jaelee

honey
মধু
modhoo

lemon
লেবু
layboo

ice-cream
আইস্ক্রীম
aaeeskreem

lettuce
লেটুস
laetoos

loaf
গোটা পাউরুটি
gota paarotee

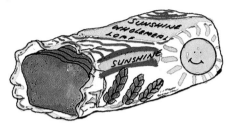

margarine
ম্যারজারিন
maarjareen

meat
মিট
meet

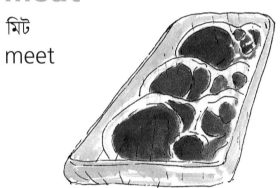

melon
তরমুজ
<u>t</u>armooz

milk
দুধ
<u>d</u>u<u>d</u>h

mushroom
মারস্রুমস্
mashroom

onion
পেঁয়াজ
payaaj

orange
কমলালেবু
kamlalayboo

33

pancake
প্যানকেইক
paenkayk

pasta
পাস্টা
paesta

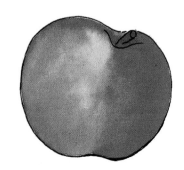

peach
পীচ্
peech

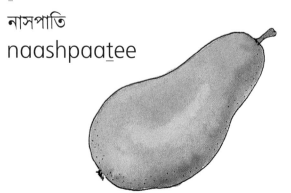

pear
নাসপাতি
naashpaatee

peas
মটরসুটি
motoshutee

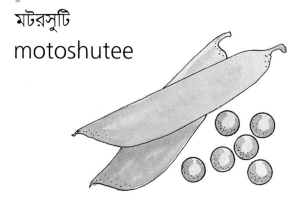

pepper
গোলমরিচ
mirch

pickle
আচার
aachaar

picnic
পিক্‌নিক
piknik

34

pie
পাই
paaee

pineapple
আনারস
anarash

pizza
পিজা
piza

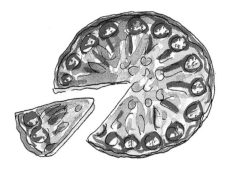

plum
প্লাম
plum

pop
পপ
pop

potato
আলু
aaloo

pudding
পুডিং
puding

rice
চাউল
chaaool

salad

স্যালাড
saalaa<u>d</u>

salt

লবন
lobon

sandwich

স্যানডুইচ
saendwich

sauce

স্যস
sos

soup

স্যূপ
soop

spaghetti

স্প্যাগেটি
spaagaetee

strawberry

স্ট্রব্যেরী
straabaree

sugar

চিনি
chini

sweets
সুইটস্
sweets

tangerine
ট্যানজারিন
taenjareen

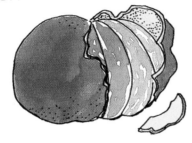

tea
চা
cha

toast
টোস্ট্
tost

tomato
টমাটো
tamaato

vegetable
শাকশব্জী
shaakshabjee

water
জল
jol

yoghurt
দই
doee

Living Creatures

জীবিত প্রাণী

jibi_to praani

beetle
কাঁচপোকা
kaanchpoka

bird
পাখী
paakhi

badger
ব্যাজার
baejar

butterfly
প্রজাপতি
projapo_ti

bear
ভালুক
bhaaluk

camel
উট
oot

cat

বেড়াল

bayrdaal

caterpillar

ক্যাটারপিলর

kaytarpilar

cow

গরু

goroo

crab

কাঁকড়া

kaankrda

crocodile

কুমীর

kumeer

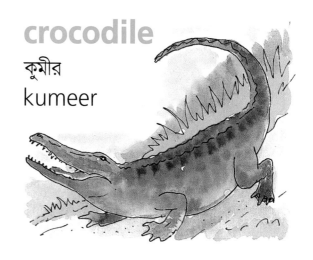

deer

হরিন

horin

dog

কুকুর

kookoor

dolphin

ডলফিন

dolfin

donkey
গাধা
gaa_dha

duck
হাঁস
haansh

eagle
ঈগল
eegal

elephant
হাতি
haa_thee

fish
মাছ
maachh

fly
মাছি
maachhi

fox
শেয়াল
shayaal

frog
ব্যাঙ
bang

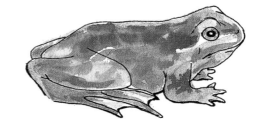

40

giraffe

জিরাফ
jiraaf

goat

ছাগল
chhagol

goldfish

সোনালী মাছ
sonaali
machh

goose

হংসী
hongshee

gorilla

গরিলা
goreela

guinea-pig

গিনিপিগ
gineepig

hedgehog

শজারু
shojaroo

hen

মুরগী
murgee

hippopotamus

জলহস্তী
jolohostee

horse

ঘোড়া
ghorda

insect

পোকা
poka

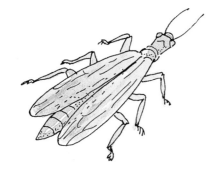

kangaroo

ক্যাঙারু
kaengaroo

ladybird

লেইডি বার্ড
laydeebard

leopard

চিতা বাঘ
chiṭa baagh

lion

সিংহ
shingho

lizard

টিকটিকি
tiktiki

lobster
গলদা চিংড়ি
gol<u>d</u>achingrdee

ostrich
উটপাখী
ooth paakhi

monkey
বানর
baanor

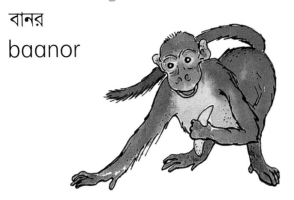

owl
পেঁচা
payncha

mouse
ইঁদুর
eedoor

panda
পান্ডা
paanda

octopus
অক্টোপাস
aaktopas

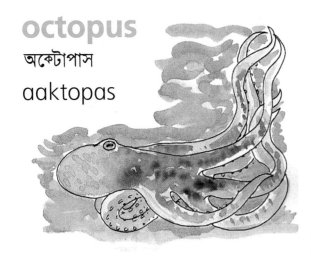

parrot
তোতাপাখী
<u>t</u>o<u>t</u>a paakhi

penguin
পেনগুইন
paengooin

sheep
ভেড়া
bhirda

rabbit
খরগোস
khargosh

snail
শামুক
shaamukh

rhinoceros
গন্ডার
gon<u>d</u>aar

snake
সাপ
shaap

shark
হাংগর
haangor

spider
মাকড়শা
maakorsha

squirrel
কাঠবিড়ালি
kaathbhirdaalee

swan
রাজহাঁস
raajhansh

tiger
বাঘ
baagh

tortoise
কচ্ছপ
kachhap

wasp
বোলতা
bolṯa

whale
তিমি
ṯimi

wolf
নেকড়ে
naykray

zebra
জেব্রা
zaybra

Plants

গাছপালা

gaachhpaala

daffodil
ডেফোডিল
daefodil

daisy
ডেইজি
dayzee

bush
ঝোপ
jhop

flower
ফুল
fool

cactus
কেকটাস্
kaektas

forest
বড় বন
baardobon

grass

ঘাস

ghaas

leaf

পাতা

paata

root

শেকড়

shakord

rose

গোলাপ

golaap

seaweed

সীউইড

seeweed

seed

বীচি

beechi

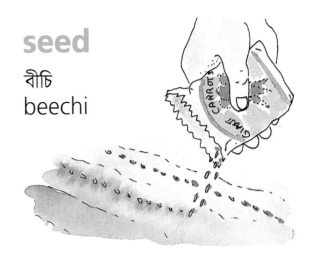

sunflower

সূর্য্যমুখী

shurjomukhi

tree

বৃক্ষ

brikho

Weather and Seasons

আবহাওয়া এবং ঋতু

aabhawa
aybongri̱tu

flood
বন্যা
bonaya

fog
কুয়াসা
kuwasha

autumn
শরৎ
shara̱t

rain
বৃষ্টি
brishtee

cloud
মেঘ
maygh

rainbow
রামধেনু
raam̱dhanoo

sky
আকাশ
aakaash

snow
তুষার
tooshar

spring
বসন্ত
boshanto

storm
ঝড়
jhord

summer
গ্রীষ্ম
grisho

sun
সূর্য্য
surjo

wind
বাতাস
baataash

winter
শীত
sheeth

Natural Features

প্রাকৃতিক বৈশিষ্ট্য

prakritik
boeeshishthya

cave
গুহা
guha

cliff
দুরারোহ পর্বত
durarho
parba<u>t</u>

desert
মরুভূমি
moorobhoomi

earthquake
ভূমিকম্প
bhoomikampo

island
দ্বীপ
<u>d</u>weep

lake
সরোবর
sharobar

mountain
পাহাড়
pahard

river
নদী
na<u>d</u>i

sand
বালি
baali

sea
সমুদ্র
shamu<u>d</u>ara

soil
মাটি
maatee

volcano
আগ্নেয়গিরি
aagniogiri

waterfall
জলপ্রপাত
jaalopropa<u>t</u>

waves
ঢেউ
dhayoo

Space

মহাকাশ

mahaakaash

moon
চাঁদ
chaand

rocket
রকেট
raaket

comet
কমেট
komat

satellite
সেটেলাইট
saetaylaaeet

Earth
পৃথিবী
prithibee

stars
তারা
taara

People at Work

নানারকমের কাজ

nanarokamyr kaaj

acrobat
দড়াবাজিকর
daurda-baajikor

artist
শিল্পী
shilpee

baker
রুটিওয়ালা
rooteewala

builder
রাজমিস্ত্রি
raajmis_tree

businessman
ব্যবসায়ী
baebshaaee

butcher
কসাই
koshaaee

carpenter

ছুতোর

choot̲or

cook

রাধুনী

raad̲hunee

dentist

দন্ত চিকিৎসক

d̲aant̲o
chikit̲shak

diver

ডুবুরী

dooboori

doctor

ডাক্তার

daaktar

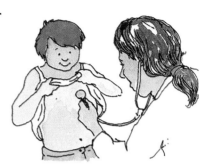

electrician

ইলেকট্রিসিয়ান

ilaektreesheean

farmer

কৃষক

krishak

fire-fighter

দমকলকর্মী

domalkormi

fisherman

ধীবর

dheebar

lorry driver

লরী ড্রাইভার

laaree draaeevar

gardener

মালী

maali

mechanic

মেকানিক

makaynik

hairdresser

হেয়ার ড্রেসার

hayardreasar

musician

গায়ক

gaayak

judge

জাজ

jaj

nurse

নার্স

nars

people

জনসাধারণ

jaanoshaadaron

policewoman

পুলিশওম্যান

poleeswoman

pilot

পাইলট

paailat

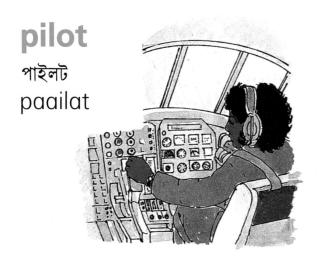

postman

পিয়ন

peeon

plumber

প্লামার

plamar

sailor

নাবিক

naabik

policeman

পুলিশম্যান

poleesmaen

scientist

বৈজ্ঞানিক

boigiaanik

secretary
সেক্রেটারী
saekraytaree

shopkeeper
দোকানী
dukaanee

soldier
সৈনিক
shoinik

teacher
শিক্ষক
shikhak

train driver
ট্রেইন ড্রাইভার
trayn
draaeevar

vet
পশু চিকিৎসক
poshu
chikiṯshak

waiter
খাদ্য পরিবেশক
khadho
paribayshak

waitress
খাদ্য পরিবেশিকা
khadho
paribayshika

Places we Visit

আমাদের দর্শনীয় জায়গা

aamaa<u>d</u>ayr <u>d</u>arshaneeon jaayga

cinema
সিনেমা
sinayma

factory
কারখানা
kaarkhana

bank
ব্যাংক
baenk

farm
ফার্ম
faarm

church
চার্চ
charch

fire station
ফায়ার স্টেশন
faair stayshan

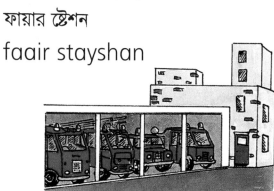

hospital

হস্পিটাল
haaspital

hotel

হোটেল
hotal

library

লাইব্রেরী
laaibrayree

market

মার্কেট
maarket

mosque

মসজিদ
mosji<u>d</u>

museum

যাদুঘর
jaa<u>d</u>ooghar

office

অফিস
aafis

park

পার্ক
paark

police station

পুলিস স্টেশন
polees
stayshan

post office

ডাকঘর
daakghar

queue

সারিবদ্ধ
shaaribodho

restaurant

রেস্টুরেন্ট
raestoraent

school

স্কুল
skool

shop

দোকান
dukaan

sports centre

স্পোর্স সেনটার
sports
saentar

supermarket

সুপার মার্কেট
supar maarkit

Transport and Communications

যানবাহন ও যাতায়াতের পথ

jaanbaahon o jaataytar path

aeroplane
বিমান
biman

airport
এয়ারপোর্ট
ayarport

ambulance
এ্যাম্বুলেনস্
aemboolaens

balloon
ব্যালুন
baaloon

barge
বজরা
bojra

bicycle
বাইসাইকেল
baaeesikal

boat
নৌকা
nouka

bridge
সেতু
shay_too

bus
বাস
bas

canoe
ক্যানু
kaanoo

car
কার
kaar

caravan
ক্যারাভ্যেন
kaeravaan

car park
কার পার্ক
kaar paark

coach
কোচ
koch

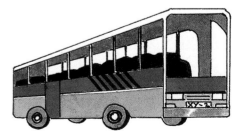

engine
এন্জিন
injin

envelope
খাম
khaam

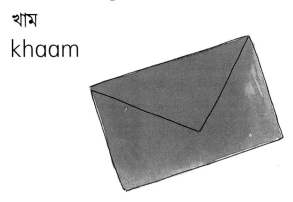

fax machine
ফ্যাক্স মেসিন
faeks masheen

ferry
ফেরী
fayree

fire-engine
ফায়ার ইন্জিন
faair injin

helicopter
হেলিকপটর
haelikoptar

letter
চিঠি
chithee

TO GRANDMA.

lift
লিফট
lift

LIFT

lighthouse

লাইট হাউস্

laaeet
haaoos

oar

দাঁড়

<u>d</u>aard

lorry

লরী

laaree

parachute

প্যারাসুট

paeraashoot

motorbike

মটরবাইক

motarbaaeek

parcel

পারসেল

paarsal

motorway

মটরওয়ে

motarway

passenger

যাত্রী

yaa<u>t</u>ri

petrol pump

পেট্রল পাম্প
paetrol pamp

platform

প্ল্যাটফর্ম
plaetfaarm

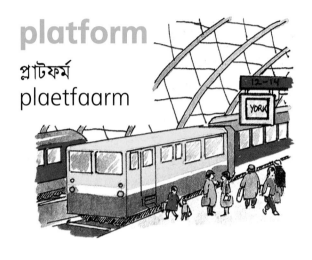

police car

পুলিশ কার
polees kaar

racing car

রেসিং কার
raysing kaar

road

রাস্তা
raasta

ship

জাহাজ
jahaaj

stamp

ডাকটিকিট
daaktikit

station

স্টেশন
stayshan

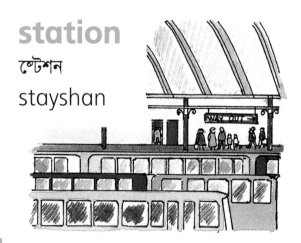

submarine
সাবমেরিন
sabmayreen

tanker
টেংকার
taenkar

taxi
টেক্সি
taeksee

telephone
টেলিফোন
taeleefon

telephone box
টেলিফোন বকস
taeleefon baaks

ticket
টিকিট
tikit

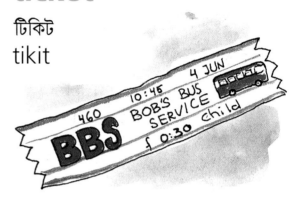

tractor
ট্রাকটর
traektar

traffic lights
ট্রাফিক লাইট
traeffik laaeet

trailer
ট্রেইলর
traylar

train
রেলগাড়ী
raylgaardi

tunnel
সুরংগ
shuranga

van
ভ্যান
vaen

wagon
ওয়াগ্যন
waegan

wheel
চাকা
chaaka

wheelchair
হুইল চেয়ার
weel
chayar

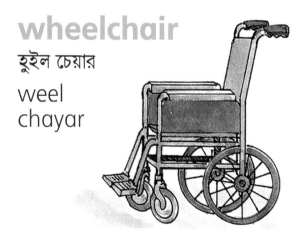

yacht
ইওট্
yaat

Tools and Machines

যন্ত্রপাতি ও মেসিন

jan_tropaa_ti o masheen

calculator
ক্যালকুলেটর
kaelkoolaytar

camera
ক্যামেরা
kaemra

computer
কম্পিউটার
kampeeootar

crane
ক্রেইন
krayn

digger
ডিগার
digar

drill
ড্রিল
dril

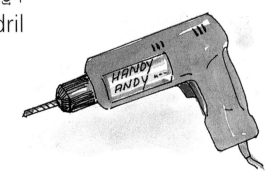

hammer

হামার
haemar

sewing machine

সেলাইর মেসিন
silaaeer masheen

rake

রেইক
rayk

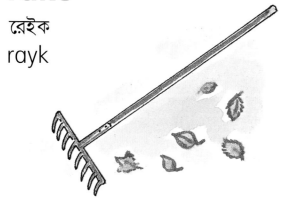

spade

কোদাল
kudaal

saw

করাত
koraat

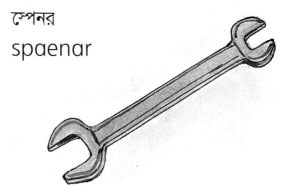

spanner

স্পেনর
spaenar

screwdriver

স্কু ড্রাইভার
skroo draaeevar

typewriter

টাইপ রাইটর
taaeep raaeetar

Toys, Games and Musical Instruments

খেলনা, খেলা ও বাদ্য যন্ত্র

khaylna,
khayla o
baadho jantro

ball

বল
baal

balloon

ব্যালুন
baaloon

bat

ব্যাট
baet

bicycle

বাইসাইকেল
baaeesikal

bricks

ব্রিকস্
briks

cards

কার্ডস্
kaardz

chess
দাবাখেলা
daabakhaela

comic
কমিক
komik

crayons
ক্রেয়নস্
krayonz

cricket
ক্রিকেট
krikit

dancing
নাচা
naacha

dice
ছক্কা
chhakka

draughts
ড্রাফ্টস্
draafts

drum
ড্রাম
drum

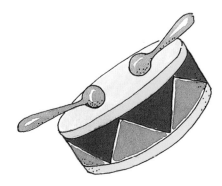

flute
বাঁশী
baanshi

football
ফুটবল
futbaal

golf
গল্‌ফ
golf

guitar
গিটার
gitar

gymnastics
জিমনাস্টিক
jimnaastik

harp
হারপ্
haarp

horse riding
ঘোড়ায় চড়া
ghurdaaee chorda

jigsaw
জিকসো
jigsaa

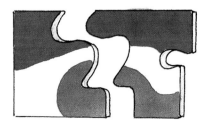

jumping

লাফ দেওয়া
laaf<u>d</u>aywa

kite

ঘুড়ি
ghurdee

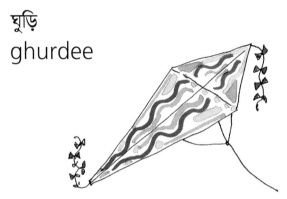

mask

মুখোস
mukosh

paintbrush

পেইন্টব্রাস
payntbursh

paints

পেইন্টস্
paynts

piano

পিয়ানো
peeaano

puppet

পুতুল
pu<u>t</u>ul

recorder

রেকরডার
rikaardar

roller boots
রোলার বুটস্
rolar boots

seesaw
সী-সো
seesaaw

roundabout
রাউন্ড এবাউট
raaoond
abaaoot

skipping-rope
স্কীপিং রোপ
skiping rope

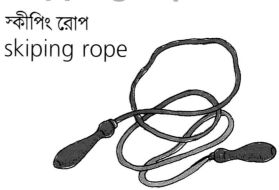

rounders
রাউন্ডার
raaoondarz

slide
স্লাইড
slaaeed

running
দৌড়ানো
daurdno

swimming
সাঁতার দেওয়া
shatar daywa

swing
দোলনা
<u>d</u>olna

table tennis
টেবিল টেনিস
taybal taenis

tambourine
ট্যামব্যরীন
taembooreen

tennis
টেনিস
taenis

trombone
ট্রমবৌন
trombon

trumpet
ট্রামপিট
trumpat

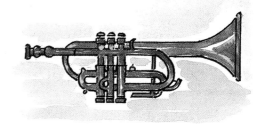

violin
ভায়লিন
vaailin

xylophone
জাইলোফোন
zaaeelofon

Fantasy and Imagination

উদ্ভট খেয়াল এবং কল্পনা

u̱thbhot̲ khayal
abang kalpana

castle
দুর্গ
d̲urgo

circus
সার্কাস
sarkas

angel
দেবদূত
d̲aybdoot̲

clown
ভাঁড়
bhaard

cannon
কামান
kamaan

crown
মুকুট
mukut

dragon
দানব
d̲aanab

ghost
ভুত
bhoo̲th

giant
দৈত্য
d̲oit̲o

king
রাজা
raaja

magician
যাদুকর
jaad̲ookar

monster
মনস্টার
maanstar

palace
প্রাসাদ
prashad̲

pirate
জলদস্যু।।
jalad̲ayshya

prince
রাজপুত্র
raajputra

princess
রাজকন্যা
raajkanya

prison
কারাগার
karagaar

queen
রানী
raani

sword
তলোয়ার
talwaar

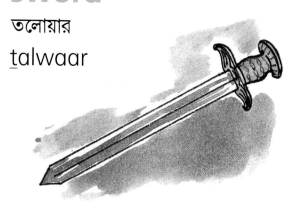

treasure
ধনদৌলত
dhandolat

witch
ডাইনী
daainee

wizard
মায়াবী
maayabee

Numbers and Shapes

সংখ্যা ও আকার

shonka o aakar

one
এক
aek

two
দুই
dooi

three
তিন
t̲in

four
চার
chaar

five
পাঁচ
paanch

six
ছয়
chhoay

seven
সাত
shaat̲

eight
আট
aath

nine
নয়
noay

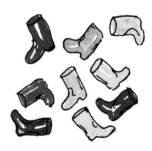

ten
দশ
d̲osh

eleven
এগারো
aegaaro

sixteen
ষোল
sholo

twelve
বারো
baaro

seventeen
সতেরো
shotayro

thirteen
তেরো
tayro

eighteen
আঠারো
aathaaro

fourteen
চৌদ্দ
chaudo

nineteen
উনিশ
unees

fifteen
পনেরো
puneero

twenty
কুড়ি
kurdee

circle
বৃত্ত
britho

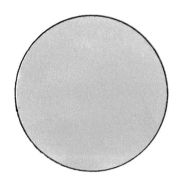

cube
কিউব
kioob

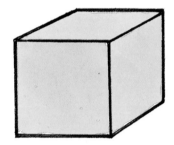

cylinder
সিলিনডার
silindar

diamond
ডায়মন্ড
daayamand

oval
ডিম্বাকার
dimbakaar

rectangle
রেকট্যাংগল
raektaengal

square
বর্গক্ষেত্র
bargokhaytro

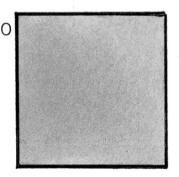

triangle
ত্রিভুজ
tribhooj

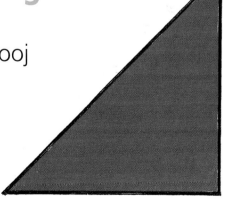

Time

সময়

shomoy

Monday

সোমবার
shombar

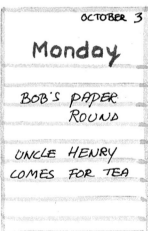

Tuesday

মঙ্গলবার
mangalbar

Wednesday

বুধবার
budhbar

Thursday

বৃহস্পতিবার
brishpatibar

Friday

শুক্রবার
shukarobar

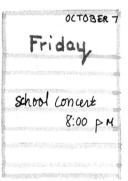

Saturday

শনিবার
shonibar

Sunday

রবিবার
robibar

January
জানুয়ারী
janwaree

February
ফেব্রুয়ারী
farwaree

March
মার্চ
maarch

April
এপ্রিল
aypral

May
মে
mai

June
জুন
joon

July
জুলাই
joolaaee

August
আগস্ট
aagast

September
সেপটেম্বর
sitambar

October
অক্টোবর
aktoobar

November
নভেম্বর
navambar

December
ডিসেম্বর
disambar

daytime
দিনের বেলা
dinayr bayla

afternoon
বিকেল
bikhayl

night-time
রাত
raat

evening
সন্ধ্যা
shondya

morning
সকাল
shokaal

sunrise
সূর্যোদয়
shurjodway

midday
দুপুর
dupoor

sunset
সূর্যস্ত
shurjoasto

o'clock

সাতটা বাজে
saata bajay

breakfast

প্রাতরাশ
praatoraash

half-past

সাড়ে এগারোটা
shaarday agarota

lunch

মধ্যাহ্নভোজ
mudhnobhoj

quarter-past

সোয়া
shawa

tea

জলখাবার
jalkhabar

quarter to

পৌনে
paunay

supper

নৈশভোজ
nushobhoj

Colours

রং

raang

black
কালো
kaalo

blue
নীল
neel

brown
বাদামী
badaami

green
সবুজ
shaybooj

gold
সোনালী
shonaali

silver
রুপালী
rupaali

grey
ধূসর
dhushor

orange
কমলা
kamola

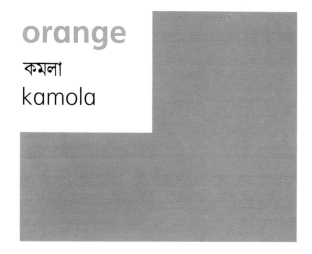

pink
গোলাপী
gulaapi

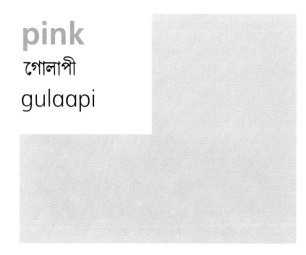

purple
বেগুনী
bayguni

red
লাল
laal

violet
গাড় বেগুনী
gar_do bayguni

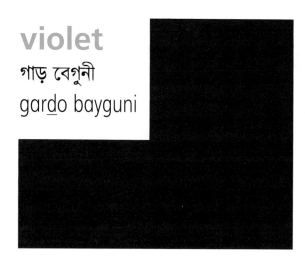

white
সাদা
sha_da

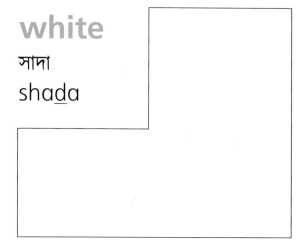

yellow
হলুদ
holu_dh

Adjectives

বিশেষণ

bishayshan

back
পেছনে
pichhanay

front
সামনে
shaamnay

clean
পরিষ্কার
porishkaar

dirty
নোংরা
nongra

cold
ঠান্ডা
thanda

hot
গরম
goram

empty
খালি
khaali

full
ভর্তি
bhur_ti

fast
দ্রুত
_dru_to

slow
ধীরে
_dheeray

happy
খুশী
khushi

sad
দু:খিত
_dukhi_to

heavy
ভারী
bhaari

light
হাল্কা
halka

large
বৃহৎ
brihot

small
ছোট
chhoto

long
লম্বা
lamba

short
খাট
khaato

narrow
সরু
shoroo

wide
চওড়া
chaurda

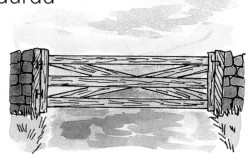

old
বুড়ো
boordo

young
কচি
kochi

Word list

Aa

acrobat	53
aeroplane	61
afternoon	84
airport	61
ambulance	61
angel	76
ankle	4
apple	29
April	83
apron	4
arm	4
artist	53
August	83
autumn	48

Bb

baby	14
back	4, 88
badge	4
badger	38
baker	53
ball	70
balloon	61, 70
banana	29
bandage	14
bank	58
barge	61
bat	70
bath	14
battery	14
bear	38
bed	14
beetle	38
bell	14
belt	4
bicycle	61, 70
bird	38
biscuit	29

black	86
blouse	5
blue	86
boat	62
book	15
boots	5
bottle	15
bowl	15
boy	15
bread	29
breakfast	85
bricks	70
bridge	62
brother	15
brown	86
brush	15
bucket	15
buckle	5
builder	53
bus	62
bush	46
businessman	53
butcher	53
butter	29
butterfly	38
buttons	5

Cc

cabbage	29
cactus	46
cake	30
calculator	68
calendar	15
camel	38
camera	68
cannon	76
canoe	62
cap	5
car	62
caravan	62
cardigan	5

cards	70
car park	62
carpenter	54
carpet	16
carrot	30
castle	76
cat	39
caterpillar	39
cauliflower	30
cave	50
cereal	30
chair	16
chapatti	30
cheek	5
cheese	30
cherry	30
chess	71
chest	5
children	16
chimney	16
chin	6
chocolate	30
church	58
cinema	58
circle	81
circus	76
clean	88
cliff	50
clock	16
cloud	48
clown	76
coach	62
coat	6
coffee	31
cold	88
comet	52
comic	71
computer	68
cook	54
cooker	16
cow	39
crab	39

Hh

hair	7
hairdresser	55
half-past	85
hamburger	32
hammer	69
hand	7
handkerchief	7
happy	89
harp	72
hat	8
head	8
heavy	89
hedgehog	41
helicopter	63
helmet	8
hen	41
hippopotamus	42
honey	32
hook	19
horse	42
horse riding	72
hose	19
hospital	59
hot	88
hotel	59
house	19

Ii

ice-cream	32
insect	42
iron	19
island	50

Jj

jacket	8
jam	32
January	83
jeans	8
jelly	32
jigsaw	72
judge	55
jug	19

July	83
jumper	8
jumping	73
June	83

Kk

kangaroo	42
kettle	20
key	20
king	77
kite	73
knee	8
knife	20

Ll

laces	8
ladder	20
ladybird	42
lake	50
lamp	20
large	90
lawn	20
leaf	47
leg	9
lemon	32
leopard	42
letter	63
lettuce	32
library	59
lift	63
light	89
light bulb	20
lighthouse	64
lion	42
lips	9
lizard	42
loaf	33
lobster	43
long	90
lorry	64
lorry driver	55
lunch	85

Mm

magazine	20
magician	77
man	21
March	83
margarine	33
market	59
mask	73
match	21
May	83
meat	33
mechanic	55
medicine	21
melon	33
microwave	21
midday	84
milk	33
mirror	21
Monday	82
money	21
monkey	43
monster	77
Months of the year:	83
moon	52
morning	84
mosque	59
mother	21
motorbike	64
motorway	64
mountain	51
mouse	43
mouth	9
mug	21
museum	59
mushroom	33
musician	55

Nn

nail	9
narrow	90
neck	9
necklace	9
needle	22
newspaper	22

A First Bilingual Dictionary

English/Bengali

ISBN 0-7217-9500-5

9 780721 795003

SCHOFIELD & SIMS LTD., HUDDERSFIELD, ENGLAND

EXAM *Revision* NOTES

AS/A-LEVEL
German

Thomas Reimann

2nd Edition

PHILIP ALLAN
UPDATES